GREENHO
FOR BE(

LEARN THE MOST POPULAR VEGETABLES AND FRUITS TO GROW IN A GREENHOUSE

By Beverly Hill

Introduction

I want to thank you and congratulate you for choosing the book, *"GREENHOUSE GUIDE FOR BEGINNERS: Learn the Most Popular Vegetables and Fruits to Grow in a Greenhouse".*

This book contains proven steps and strategies on how to prepare vegetables and fruits for growing in a greenhouse.

Anyone who can garden in their backyard can transition to gardening in a greenhouse. Greenhouse gardening offers many advantages, including being able to grow all year long, keeping favorite plants alive all through the winter, and starting seeds more easily. You must purchase special equipment, and apply certain methods to garden successfully in a greenhouse, but they are well worth the effort.

If you're thinking about making a personal greenhouse for your own garden, but just don't have any experience with how to plan one out, or build it, not to fear, this book is going to point out some of the most important points to consider in the process. Think of it as a greenhouse for beginners guide. In the first chapter I've listed some of the more common questions and considerations that most people ask me about when starting a garden greenhouse project.

Thanks again for choosing this book, I hope you enjoy it!

© **Copyright 2017 by Holistic Measures, LLC - All rights reserved.**

This document is geared towards providing exact and reliable information in regards to the topic and issue covered. The publication is sold with the idea that the publisher is not required to render accounting, officially permitted, or otherwise, qualified services. If advice is necessary, legal or professional, a practiced individual in the profession should be ordered.

- From a Declaration of Principles which was accepted and approved equally by a Committee of the American Bar Association and a Committee of Publishers and Associations.

In no way is it legal to reproduce, duplicate, or transmit any part of this document in either electronic means or in printed format. Recording of this publication is strictly prohibited and any storage of this document is not allowed unless with written permission from the publisher. All rights reserved.

The information provided herein is stated to be truthful and consistent, in that any liability, in terms of inattention or otherwise, by any usage or abuse of any policies, processes, or directions contained within is the solitary and utter responsibility of the recipient reader. Under no circumstances will any legal responsibility or blame be held against the publisher for any reparation, damages, or monetary loss due to the information herein, either directly or indirectly.

Respective authors own all copyrights not held by the publisher.

The information herein is offered for informational purposes solely, and is universal as so. The presentation of the information is without contract or any type of guarantee assurance.

The trademarks that are used are without any consent, and the publication of the trademark is without permission or backing by the trademark owner. All trademarks and brands within this book are for clarifying purposes only and are the owned by the owners themselves, not affiliated with this document.

ABOUT THE AUTHOR

Beverly Hill is a sociologist. She is the CEO of C.E.F Associates and formerly served as head of department of sociology in Premier Natural Resources Inc.

A graduate of Nelson High School also graduated from the University of Toronto with a B.A in economics and finance and holds an M.S from Cambridge University in public relations and PhD in sociology.

She has written many articles on human equality, animal rights, environmental issues, personal development and peace keeping in different newspapers. She has also appeared in many magazines and is frequently interviewed for articles on family, race, socioeconomic status, and how to survive in your environment. She has also worked on the importance of health of relationship between parents and children. Her book 'The Middle Child' focuses on the importance of the attention given to the children and what to expect from them. This book helps parents understand their children.

In addition to these works she is also the author of 'Surviving Alone ' which is about her own childhood growing up; she writes about her family struggles living on a low income budget and growing her own food to survive.

C.E.F Associates formed in 1999 in Idaho, USA she worked both nationally and internationally. This is a consulting company which has clients all over the world. Ms. Hill the CEO of the company is the main reason of the huge client base because of her servings in foreign countries.

TABLE OF CONTENT

Introduction

Chapter 1

GREENHOUSE SIZE

Chapter 2

GROWING A GREENHOUSE ORGANIC VEGETABLE GARDEN

Chapter 3

WHY GROW IN A GREENHOUSE

Chapter 4

THE GREENHOUSE ADVANTAGE

Chapter 5

HOW TO GROW VEGETABLES IN A GREENHOUSE

Chapter 6

AIR CIRCULATION IN THE GREENHOUSE

Conclusion

Preview Of 'HERB GARDENING: HOW TO GROW YOUR OWN HERBS'

Chapter 1

HERBAL GARDENING

Chapter 1

GREENHOUSE SIZE

Generally speaking, the size of your greenhouse will automatically be limited by the space available to construct it upon. That seems obvious I know, but you'd be surprised at how many people miss this first step. You should have sufficient space to accommodate all the plants you want to grow and then some! There should be enough space for walkways and benches with some flexibility for scaling up the operation in the future if so desired, and trust me; you'll fill out that initial space in no time flat!

One important tip to utilize in the beginning is to incorporate hanging rods in the house wherever possible to accommodate hanging baskets. Also, ensure that structural capabilities are set up to handle the installation of growing lamps and side wall shelves. Again, it's really the key to choose a structure that allows you the flexibility to add-on to the original structure if you are a serious grower, and feel that you would need more growing room later.

HOW MUCH TIME TO SPEND ON YOUR GREENHOUSE

A greenhouse for beginners, even a small hobby house, requires that you spend time in it on a regular basis. Of course, there is some flexibility in this, but you do need to make room in your schedule to putter around in your greenhouse frequently. When you set out to build your greenhouse, be honest and realistic with yourself about how much time you're going to be able to dedicate to this new gardening venture. Making plans that are to grandiose will end up costing you heavily down the road.

LOCAL LAWS AND GUIDELINES

Generally, the area of the country you live in will have its own set of laws and guidelines relating to building a structure like this. You may need to obtain permits, and show compliance with construction guidelines, especially if your greenhouse is to be classifies as a permanent structure. It would be a good idea to confirm whether construction of a greenhouse on your property would make you liable to pay additional taxes.

For the most part, small greenhouses won't be on the hook for this, but it's always wise to make sure just in case. All you have to do is approach the local authorities in your area that are responsible, and find out what clearances you'll need before you start any kind of construction.

THINGS TO CONSIDER WHEN PREAPARING FOR YOUR GREENHOUSE

You need to plan for other things as well, like the cost of heating, irrigation, and ventilation cost. If you reside in a particularly cold winter region, you need to consider the costs associated with electrical or propane heating. Will you be able to afford it, or will you need to cut down the size of your house so these heating costs won't become prohibitive?

Your choice of covering material needs to be considered as it relates to monetary investment and suitability. It's also important to think about how much it will cost to irrigate the greenhouse. How far the structure is from the home will dictate this because the further away it is the more involved it will be to set up the proper watering system.

Chapter 2

GROWING A GREENHOUSE ORGANIC VEGETABLE GARDEN

There are many advantages to growing organic vegetables in a greenhouse. Although you won't automatically be weed and pest free just because you are growing indoors, you will have complete control over how you protect your precious organic plants. Lean to greenhouses are especially well adapted to an organic garden, as you can place them close to your kitchen door. Because lean-tos are attached to a structure, there are only three glazed sides. This makes them energy efficient because warm and cool temperatures can be diverted from your home through the common wall your home shares with the attached lean to.

Here are tips for producing healthy and delicious organic fruits and vegetables for your kitchen garden.

AVOID GREENHOUSES MADE FROM SYNTHETIC MATERIALS

Many side panels are now made from various types of plastics and polycarbonates, but true organic aficionados opt for glass greenhouses. The panel is even more important than the frame because moisture will collect on the panel's surface, and drip on your garden.

PLAN YOUR VEGETABLE GARDEN LAYOUT IN ADVANCE

Using graph paper, plot where you will place each plant in your greenhouse. Although "companion planting" is not a new concept, the use of it in an organic greenhouse cannot be over emphasized. Greenhouse gardening has its own share of pest problems, many which can be avoided naturally by the use of companion planting.

1) Nasturtiums chase away aphid.

2) Onions and Leeks planted next to carrots deter carrot fly.

3) French Marigolds next to tomatoes will ward off greenfly and black fly.

4) An Elder shrub can deter mice.

5) If you plant directly into the ground, ants can be a problem. Plant Peppermint, Spearmint, Bay Leaf or Garlic to chase away those little critters.

6) And of course, for snails and slugs there is the ever popular beer trap. Their attraction to the fragrance of

beer is their downfall. A little sip, they'll get drunk and drown.

7) On the other hand, to attract healthy bugs, plant Buddleia, Achilles and flowering herbs such as Dill, Rosemary and Lavender throughout your greenhouse. These will attract pest-devouring ladybirds, lacewings and hoverflies.

Start with organic soil. Don't skimp on the quality of the soil. or the organic additives you'll add to your soil like compost, manure. or sea products like kelp. Additives are like fertilizer, they boost the health of your soil. Remember, additives vary depending on what plants you grow. Different plants have different needs.

Be careful. If you plant taller vegetables and fruits such as tomatoes. or corn directly into the ground make sure they have plenty of ceiling space to grow to their full height. Also. you must be certain that the soil is free from dangerous organisms and toxins. If you suspect your soil contains toxins, purchase a soil test kit from your seed supplier.

Another option is to sterilize your soil. Put your desired amount of soil in an over roasting bag; add enough water to dampen the soil and tie it shut. Poke a meat thermometer through the bag, and heat in a 200 degree oven. Keep the temperature of the soil as close to 170 degrees as possible for 30 minutes. The temperature of the soil won't reach the temperature of the oven within 30 minutes, but it's best to keep an eye on the thermometer. If it gets too warm simply turn the oven down, or even off if you are nearing the end of the 30 minutes cycle. Put the cooled sterilized soil into pots, and sink them directly into the ground.

COMPOST

This is the most important and most affordable factor in your vegetable garden.

Remember to keep your compost organic. That means everything you toss in there has to be organic. If you put anything that contains chemicals into your compost bin, your compost will contain chemicals.

Control weeds before they grow. Lay a 1" to 2" thickness of newspaper on top of the soil, and cover with about the same amount of soil or mulch. It's not an exact science. The thinker the paper, the more it will deter the weeds. Most newspaper inks are soy-based so your little plants will stay happy and healthy. Do not use the glossy color inserts as they are not only very toxic, water cannot penetrate the glossy surface. Plain old newspaper however, will work wonders. It will also decompose over time, and be a healthy additive to your soil.

KNOW YOUR NATURAL HERBICIDES

If an extreme bug infestation heists, and you find you need an herbicide, a tried and true method is the use of an organic soap mixture. Buy the cheapest type of lemon dish soap you can find. The cheap brands will usually not have a lot of the toxic additives that the more costly labels use. Mix one tablespoon of the soap into a gallon of water and pour into a sprayer. Apply liberally on top and bottom of the leaves. Re-apply every one or two weeks. The soap mixture has the added benefit of reducing the risk of various diseases that can develop.

PULL SPENT PLANTS FROM THE SOIL

After you harvest your fruits and vegetables, pull them from the soil, and toss them in your compost bin for next year's garden. Removing spent plants from the soil helps maintain the nutrients in the soil, and discourage pests.

Buy a cookbook! Get yourself a good organic fruit and vegetable cookbook and enjoy your harvest!

Chapter 3

WHY GROW IN A GREENHOUSE

Each year as the autumnal equinox passes us by, day-length dwindles to an increasingly noticeable degree. By the winter solstice, it becomes too cold and dark in many regions for much of anything to grow in the field. But greenhouse growers are gearing up to start tomato, lettuce, eggplant and pepper seeds, or other carefully chosen vegetables, herbs, and flowers. The seedlings may be started, or transplanted into a heated or unheated greenhouse or hoop-house, depending on the latitude, crop, and a host of additional variables unique to the greenhouse grower's operation.

If working in the greenhouse sounds like an antidote for the midwinter blues, not to mention a way to make some year-round cash then read on to learn more about how greenhouse growing might fit into your business plan.

Chapter 4

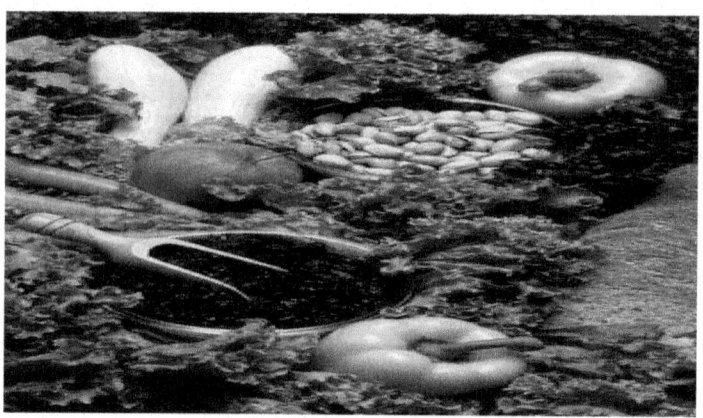

THE GREENHOUSE ADVANTAGE

The obvious reason to grow greenhouse vegetables, flowers, and herbs is to have crops at a time of year when they can't be grown outdoors. Out-of-season tomatoes, cucumbers, peppers, eggplant, lettuce, basil, and other vegetables command high prices in some markets. It is important to note, though, the cost of winter production of warm-weather crops like tomatoes is very high, so prepare to jump into it only once you are certain you have a market, and a price that will provide a return on your investment. Heating will be your biggest cost, followed by labor.

And if you intend to remain in production through the very coldest, shortest winter months, you may also need to provide supplemental lighting-particularly during a long spell of overcast weather.

If you have never attempted to grow greenhouse vegetables in the winter, you should do a great deal of preliminary research to determine whether it can be profitable for you, given your climate, greenhouse structure, and fuel costs. Fortunately, there are many freely available resources to help you calculate costs and potential returns. An internet search for greenhouse tomatoes enterprise budget, for example, will return a lengthy list of references to inform your research. Look for those published by your regional universities and cooperative extension agencies.

For predicting heating costs, an invaluable tool called Virtual Grower, is available through the USDA. This free software program prompts the user to enter information such as, nearest weather station (from which it calculates average weather conditions), type of greenhouse structure, condition of the structure, type of heating system, and price of fuel.

As for timing, the broad rule of thumb for a beginning grower in the northern half of the US or Canada, is not to plant into a greenhouse until February 15th, because the low light conditions earlier than that make the crop a riskier venture. More experienced growers and southern growers, however, can produce all winter. By mid February, many crops can be grown with only minimal heat, and still provide a month or more of earliness compared to field crops.

If you have a market where you can sell vegetables in spring, greenhouse production can be profitable, especially when combined with early field crops. You may, for example, have field-grown spinach ready in April, but that's hardly enough to fill a market stand. If, however, you can also bring head lettuce from the heated greenhouse, and arugula, radishes, and carrots from the unheated hoop-house, you're ready to put on a good display. Alternatively, think about the possibilities for Mother's Day: greenhouse tomatoes, cucumbers, cut flowers, and hanging baskets of flowers and fruiting strawberries, in addition to a full range of spring vegetables.

Season extension is just one of the advantages gained from greenhouse growing. Protected crops are less apt to be damaged by wind, rain, and hail, so the percentage of marketable products is higher. Yield is often higher as well, if you can provide optimum growing conditions for each crop. Greenhouses protect crops from many diseases, particularly those that are soil-borne and splash onto plants in the rain. And greenhouse crops may be protected from common field pests. Of course, greenhouse crops have their own particular problems such as, foliar disease, aphids and whiteflies, so vigilance is still requires.

Chapter 5

HOW TO GROW VEGETABLES IN A GREENHOUSE

Before you get started in your greenhouse whether you are a preparer, or a homesteader, learning how to grow vegetables in a greenhouse is a great skill to learn. For homesteaders, you are learning more self-reliance, living more frugally, and connecting with nature by growing the food you eat. As a preparer, you are ensuring that during a shift situation, you are prepared to grow your own food better still; there is less chance of contamination from airborne infect-ants inside your controlled climate greenhouse.

Obviously, you want to grow what you and your family will actually eat. There isn't much of a reason to grow Brussels sprouts in winter if your spouse and children won't eat them, which is definitely not a problem at our house! Aside from that, what vegetables you grow inside your greenhouse will depend a lot on the size of the greenhouse itself.

The more space your greenhouse has for planting, the more options you obviously have. If your greenhouse is a small one, you are probably better off growing small plants like root vegetables (carrots and such), and herbs. However, if you have a larger greenhouse, you can grow either lots of smaller plants, or you can grow some large ones (or a combination of the two). In fact, if you build a large enough greenhouse, you can even grow some species of fruit trees, citrus fruits like Meyer lemons, and other small trees would be ideal.

Another thing to consider when choosing plants for the greenhouse is the temperature inside your greenhouse. And, if you have the basic greenhouse setup (i.e. just a greenhouse without any heaters or fans), you will need to track the temperatures inside from day to night throughout the season. You could do that tracking a couple of different ways. You can go extremely low tech, and just put a thermometer inside the greenhouse, and checking it periodically throughout the day and night. If you want to be super high-tech about it, you could get one of the weather trackers for your greenhouse. Not only will it tell you what the ambient and soil temperatures are in the greenhouse, but it will send alerts to your phone and email if temperatures go too high or too low for your settings. It will also keep track of growing conditions so you can see trends. I'm already jealous of this system.

Controlling the Temperature in Your Greenhouse now that you know the "raw" conditions of your greenhouse, you can alter them and control the situation.

By "raw" conditions, I mean the unaltered state of pressure in your greenhouse humidity ranges, and temperature differences inside the greenhouse compared to outside. If your greenhouse is retaining too much heat for what you want to grow, simply venting the structure can change the internal temperature. You can vent through the top of the greenhouse, or you can use an exhaust fan to help pull hot air out. You could also use a louvered shutter vent to let fresh air in while allowing hot air to escape.

Maybe your greenhouse isn't getting warm enough for what you want to grow. If it gets too cold, seeds won't germinate as quickly, if at all. Plants won't grow as fast, nor will they produce as much when they're colder than they should be. There are a number of ways you can fix this problem. The most obvious is of course, to add a heater.

Chapter 6

AIR CIRCULATION IN THE GREENHOUSE

Air circulation is also a necessity for healthy plants. Good air circulation strengthens the woody tissue in stems, and decreases the opportunities for fungi to attack your plants. Dense plant growth will cause issues with air circulation, so be sure you keep your plants spaced far enough apart, and keep them trimmed. A small fan will help keep air circulating throughout the greenhouse. As well as reducing the heat in your greenhouse, ventilating would also replenish the much-needed carbon dioxide for your plants. Ventilate, even if you have to add extra heat.

A good way to ventilate (and increase air circulation) is by cross-ventilating-this is, by having an opening on each end of the greenhouse, thereby, allowing air to flow through the planting area. Just be sure to protect the openings with some wire mesh so the birds, squirrels, and other critters can't get into the greenhouse and eat everything in sight. How to grow vegetables in your greenhouse? You can use your greenhouse year-round to start plants, harden plants off, or grow vegetables.

Since you can control the weather, so to speak, you have ideal conditions any time of years to germinate and propagate new plants. Plant seeds or clippings from other plants in starter pots, cardboard egg cartons, toilet paper tubers, or eggshells, when they are ready to transplant, you can put them right in the ground in your greenhouse, you could make raised beds to ensure the soil is warmer, but it is not absolutely necessary. For that matter you can always grow your veggies in separate containers. It is the same as container gardening throughout the summer, just inside the greenhouse. In fact, you could simply move your containers insider the greenhouse when the temperature begins to drop to maintain the warmth.

If you're looking to have a full run of vegetables grown in your greenhouse during winter, you're already halfway there. You now know how to monitor and control the temperature inside, and if you are already gardening outside the greenhouse, you know the basics of growing crops. You can identify these flowers because they have both the male part (anthers) that contains the pollen, and the female part (carpals) which hold the ovary.

Some examples of self-pollinators are tomatoes, peas and peppers. Pollination occurs when wind or insects knock pollen loose from the anthers. The pollen then falls into the carpals. And fertilization occurs. In your greenhouse, you may have to assist these plants by tapping the flowers, or lightly shaking the plants to be sure the pollen has a chance to get where it needs to go.

You could also use one of these sonic plant pollinators that have a vibrating head if you wanted to speed up pollination. Summer Squash 101 (via survival at home) Image Credit Open Pollinators-Plants that have separate male and female flowers need bees, or other insects to move pollen from the male flower to the female flower. Female blossoms tend to grow close to the center of the center of the plant.

Look at the base of the blossom where it meets the stem it will have a small swollen embryonic fruit at its base. Male flowers are found on long skinny stalks all along the plant. There are usually a lot more male blossom where it meets the stem it will have a small swollen embryonic fruit at its base.

Male flowers are found on long skinny stalks all along the plant. There are usually a lot more male blossoms than female, and there typically begin blooming much earlier. To hand-pollinate these types of flowers, you can use a sharp pair of garden snipers to cut the male flower off, and tap the open blossom against an open female blossom. If you are just not sure which is which, you can use a small paint brush, or cotton swabs to brush inside each flower. That way you are sure to get pollen from the male to the female flowers. Examples of plants and both flowers are squash, melons and cucumbers.

Conclusion

Thank you again for choosing this book!

The exciting time has come to enjoy the fresh salad made from my greenhouse leaf lettuce plants. The lettuce seeds started in February because seedlings and planted into their permanent containers in March. In early May I took the bigger leaves off the stem and made a delicious salad. Everyone said how soft, tender and tasty the salad was. Leaving the smaller leaves on the only taking the larger leaves off will provide a period of continuous growth on the leaf lettuce plants. These tender lettuce leaves are great for sandwiches.

Finally, if you enjoyed this book, would you be kind enough to leave a review for this book on Amazon? It'd be greatly appreciated!

Thank you and good luck!

Preview Of 'HERB GARDENING: HOW TO GROW YOUR OWN HERBS'
Chapter 1

HERBAL GARDENING

Herbs are very easy to grow with a little sunshine, soil that drains well, some watering, and a little fertilizer or compost. Herbs can be grown in pots: however, the plants always prefer to be in the ground where they can spread out. Some plants grow quite large (4-6 feet), and when placed in pots they can become stunted and can get stressed, which causes them to be very unhappy. Main Thing Necessary to Grow Herbs is to put them in the Right Place.

The main requirement for growing Herbs is growing them in the proper location. Most prefer full sun as long as regular summer temperatures don't rise above 90 degrees. If you have very warm summers, then consider planting in an area that gets morning sun and afternoon shade in the summertime, or a place that receives filtered light (such as under a tree that allows some light to pass through). Check the area several times during the day to make sure that there are at least four hours of sun. (e.g., 8 to 12, 12 to 4, or from 9 to 11 and 2 to 4)

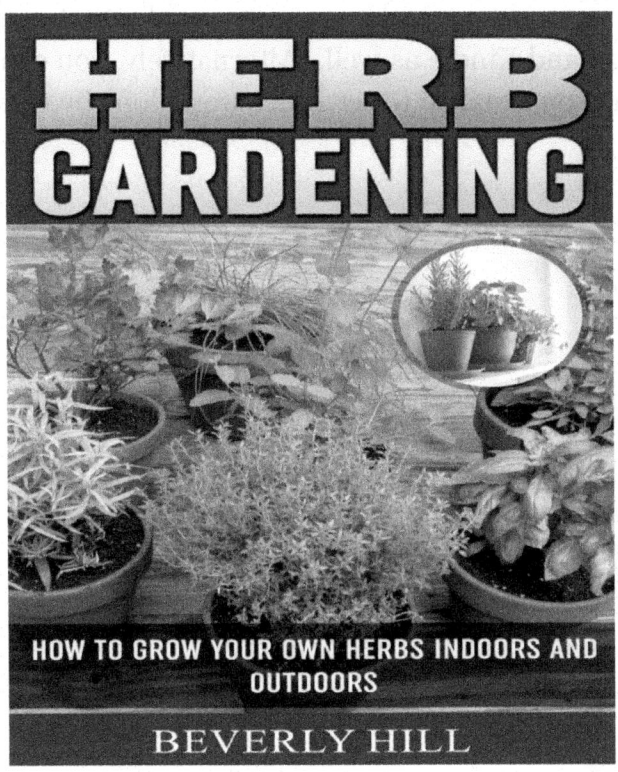

To check out the rest of (HERB GARDENING: HOW TO GROW YOUR OWN HERBS INDOORS AND OUTDOORS) on Amazon.com

Check Out My Other Books

Below you'll find some of my other popular books that are popular on Amazon and Kindle as well. Alternatively, you can visit my author page on Amazon to see other work done by me.

GREENHOUSE: HOW TO BUILD YOUR OWN GREENHOUSE.

GREENHOUSE GROWING FOR BEGINNERS: HOW TO GROW VEGETABLES AND FLOWERS.

CAMPANION PLANTING FOR BEGINNERS: LEARN WHICH PLANTS GOES WELL WITH EACH OTHER.

GROWING VEGETABLES: HOW TO GROW VEGETABLES IN CONTAINERS.

TREES: THE BEGINNERS GUIDE TO GROWING POTTED TREES.

CLEANING: DIY ALL NATURAL HOMEMADE CLEANING RECIPES FOR A SAFE AND FRIENDLY HOME.

USING HERBS FOR MEDICINE: EASY TO FOLLOW DIRECTIONS ON HOW TO USE HERBS FOR MEDICINE.

You can simply search for these titles on the Amazon website to find them.

BONUS: SUBSCRIBE TO THE FREE BOOK

Beginners Guide to Yoga & Meditation

"Stressed out? Do You Feel Like The World Is Crashing Down Around You? Want To Take A Vacation That Will Relax Your Mind, Body And Spirit? Well this Easy To Read Step By Step

E-Book Makes It All Possible!"

Instructions on how to join our mailing list, and receive a free copy of "Yoga and Meditation" can be found in any of my Kindle eBooks.

NOTES

Lightning Source UK Ltd.
Milton Keynes UK
UKOW06f1914131117
312695UK00005B/559/P